Arco Iris

Sarah Vap

saturnalia books

Distributed by University Press of New England
Hanover and London

Arco Iris

Sarah Vap

Saturnalia Books
105 Woodside Rd.
Ardmore, PA 19003
info@saturnaliabooks.com

ISBN: 978-0-9833686-4-9
Library of Congress Control Number: 2012945504

Book Design by Saturnalia Books
Printing by The Prolific Group, Canada

Cover Art: Paul Koundounaris

Distributed by:
University Press of New England
1 Court Street
Lebanon, NH 03766
800-421-1561

Grateful acknowledgment is made to the editors and staff of the following journals who published many of these poems, often in very different versions or under different titles: *Barrow Street, Bone Bouquet Journal, Caffeine Destiny, Court Green, Ensemble Jourine, Field, Fugue, Interim, La Petite Zine, Locuspoint, Pistola Mag, Skein, Slurve, 42opus.*

Thank you to Norman Dubie, Diana Park, Jenny Browne, Mark Irwin, David St. John, Anna Journey. Thank you Sean Nevin, Brian Leary, Henry Israeli, Henry Quintero, Mona Polacca, Forrest Gander, C.D. Wright, Kathy Ossip, Danielle Pafunda. For some language, thank you to Dan Beachy-Quick, Daniel Tiffany, Wade Davis, Dickinson, Baudrillard, Artaud, Levinas, and most certainly others.

For support, thank you to Arizona State University and University of Southern California, and to P.E.O. Arizona Chapter.

Heartfelt gratitude to Daniel and Jeannie Vargas and Carolina Vargas, to Gonzalo Moscoso Salazar, to Amy Savoie, and to Amir Brito Cadôr and Daniela Maura, who shared their homes and stories with us during our travels, and to Sherwin Bitsui, who wandered with us awhile.

Thank you joyfully, TF, O, M.

Contents

Ghost   1

Travel   2

Heave   3

Ghost   4

Rider   5

Ghost   6

And over her spinning rainbow   7

Travel   8

Zipaquirá Salt Mine   9

Travel   10

Travel   11

South   12

To Quito   13

History   14

Market   15

Currency   16

Thread   17

Currency   18

Traces of Eva's potato song   19

Train, Cuzco-Puno   20

Travel   21

Train, Cuzco-Puno   22

Time travel   23

The riverboat   24

Currency   25

Market   26

As if we are hemispheres folding onto each other   27

Institution, Travel   28

Travel   29

Firmament   30

Market   31

Andes   32

Hypermarket   33

Hypermarket   34

Pale   35

Covenant   36

Market   37

Sphinx   38

Learning history   39

Meridian   40

Excelling Violet   41

Excelling Violet   42

Firmament   43

Spring—   44

Iris   45

Rustling, so beautifully?   46

Galactic roses.   47

Hammer buried in white mud, bank of the Orinoco 48

Economy   49

The coca leaf fortune-teller   50

The coca leaf fortune-teller   51

Do you want to say anything here.   52

Oliviera   53

Floating turd next to the dead floating snake   54

Ghost   55

Thread   56

What we think when we travel this river   57

Firmament   58

What we think when we travel this river   59

Sunset, Tayrona   60

The seven directions   61

Night, Tayrona   62

The coca leaf fortune-teller   63

Star-shaped hubcaps across Medellín   64

Iris, starless   65

Or to say—   66

Iris   67

Ghost   68

Ruins   69

Suspension   70

Ghost   71

The coca leaf fortune-teller   72

...as water gushing forth from rock washes away that rock.

—Emmanuel Levinas

Everything that acts is cruelty.

—Antonin Artaud

Ghost

We moved pretty slowly down,

then across, then up, then across, then down.

It was hard to tell what was important.

Travel

The continent spread apart then the continent condensed around us. Like the continent, we made an effort to remember. Memory, we thought at first, was something like *pathos*—and at the infinite remove—

but memory was weight. Memory was the heavy mirror of history was shadow falling at your face—falling at your face.

Heave

We joined the tangle of heavy ghosts moaning out the strength of the patriarchs. Moaning out the impossible weight. Then we pulled the ghosts up by their chains to say: we will hurt you. We will tear you the fuck apart. We will hunt down your children we will hunt down your children's children. We will never stop the ghosts wailed.

Ghost

The road is both narrow and wide

and nobody pointed

at us or hid the mouth or whispered horror

or hallelujah as we moved by, though occasionally

they gestured to our spines as if lifting them.

As, I thought, the spines of fish are lifted clean away.

Rider

Begin with the memory of collapsing the ballerina back into the music box after she twirls in her white plastic dress slower then slower to somewhere over the rainbow. Her feet glued to the spring, she moved, I thought, as much as she possibly could. Loneliness across a whole life. Even here, in Guayaquil.

Wind from the water on my legs, my white skirt smeared with the dirt, the wine, and the lime leaf caught at your beard—we had decided to travel.

That song, also without words, played in the stateside airport as we departed. For the next few months, nearly every night, the tiny gold key clicked the box open. Unlocked the dancer—and those slowing, slowing plinks long ago to her bedroom.

Ghost

Not nostalgia not going back but as we move Lover is diminished then made of air. Once, he was even whiter he was even more sparse than that— I was, too. The long line of memory before we were born and then after—memory in other directions other shapes too—

we try to remember that far.

And over her spinning rainbow

At night we wear the double-bridle. The curb, a cold wedge of steel to the top of my throat and I submit. A snaffle presses each edge of your mouth, split to blood and very soft. Your mouth, open—fast then faster it opens—

Fuck me, or something like it I said every night. That lock, the click at that plastic bent over. He wanted to—at the spring she was glued to. The plinks, and the crank that turns her.

Travel

Sometimes we took the horse and made

ourselves some information, sometimes we took

the meaning and made ourselves some horse.

We took in, took in, to an interior shriveled

by the same old trap, cleverly set—

Zipaquirá Salt Mine

The light inside the cathedral is blue, is cut into rock—a cavern surrounded by smaller chambers. Spotlights covered with cobalt gel paper illuminate segments of the absolute darkness two hundred meters below surface.

Lick it, the tour guide says. We lick the wall of the cathedral: salt. White statues of angels in blue light but we are in the pitch-black extending backward from us—so dark we cannot see our own bodies—whatever haunts the mind of any given generation—what is mind— chambers cut into chambers

cut into light, into the black mine——. We want to join the undifferentiated ecstasy but not the general angel.

We want ecstatic mind we want the humming mind we want the hive mind arboreal mind rhizome mind mycelium mind the black chamber—the wind through it—

not the wailing mind—

Travel

The weight on the sternum—to pry it apart, to release

one single definite pressure. Then, to the one above it, the

yearslong ache at the throat.

Travel

Not the great white individual not the solitary dove

not the chorus of angels not the oblivion.

Not woman not cloud not system not the viral mind—yes, we are all one.

One buzzing remote and also inside of us one ghost thrashing one

thread of information across one continent under one blanket reaching

even into this mine, mining—reaching this siphon, siphoning—

chamber of blue lighting—when I can't get at it out there—

reach it on you mining on

you siphoning on you thrashing on you pulling—

what is it   what is it   what is it

you say again I say: salt.

South

The haunting might occur only after the demarcation—in directions we don't even know about—sometimes a light will only illuminate its own destruction. Sometimes the miner's lamp—sufficient be—to nullify the mine.

Sometimes a light is only a television on a riverboat in the Amazon—

Sometimes, we believe we are penetrating the surface to arrive—sometimes what is inside of you wants to move somewhere else and then when you least expect it will wail it will wail at your face.

To Quito

Very early morning still no light at all. Beyond the black velvet curtain of our bus named *Salve Regina*—a spark, then smoke: we live. With no wild animal. Just those two luckless cows over there that nobody knows, nobody wants to know—our moving has begun in earnest—we have moved off one hemisphere.

We have moved across one country. We are moving over this mountain. When we move we are moved inside of benevolent machines everywhere. In every machine, our window. For every window a curtain and we are on one side of it

in machines—oiled with oil from the earth over which we glide—

when our bodies move our minds, we think, and move along with them.

History

You say: transcendence is always absorbed back into the system.

You say: irreversible.

You say: even those stars.

You say: sojourn. I say: sojourn. You say: if we could but.

I say reach you say touch I say stay you say become I say respond

you say backlight I say silhouette you say ghost I say valence, fog-fluid, sight-line—

you say: say something important to me.

Market

When the rainforest unfurls from its coil around us we arrive at the market. We eat breakfast, we kiss again.

White kiss. Cuban music. Instant coffee, travel agency—you insist that our kiss be quiet. *Be this please*. Please, say something important to me, I am quiet—and left alone with this quiet trajectory— I say: what do you think about that.

You say: we won't be able to touch everything and all along.

You say: we won't be able. I say the cruelty of our common life. The ghosts, we say, are not that long line behind us.

Currency

Finally we begin to touch the people who live here. The tips of our fingers touch, or my fingers at their palms or theirs at mine. Or our arms when they hand something to me that I have asked for. When I hand something back to them.

Now I imagine how we might touch. I find more ways I want even more ways to touch—whoever you are who thinks that I don't want you—here. Take this money. Give me something beautiful you have made.

Thread

When the rainforest unfurls from its coil around us then we have unfurled from each other as when fucking in the desert we became the cave—as when fucking at the coast we rose and fell—as when fucking on the boat we were not rooted—as we move we become whatever scenery moves around us. Curtain always closed to the window.

Currency

There is a generator-operated television mounted on a steel shelf just above his hammock. There are three televisions on this level of the boat, two on the upper level—they each play a different dubbed Jean-Claude Van Damme movie over and over, at full-volume, continuously down the Amazon. The sides of these boats are open, and sometimes we pass other boats like ours also with televisions also Jean-Claude Van Damme shouting and shooting down the river. Passengers seem either to watch the screen without pause, or never once glance at it. Our boat of quiet passengers thus screams and explodes day and night while Lover slams his head over and over into its metal corner. Lover slams his head every time he leaves his hammock. Lover slams his head every time he returns. Lover slams! slams! his head at the light.

Traces of Eva's potato song

At a place between anger and anguish our beginning is cut to remembrance—at the headwaters, the slow brown water had turned bright yellow where it began to fall. A man in our boat, scar from ear to ear where someone, he told us, once slashed his throat: there, you say to him, tell us your story of the first potatoes—the star-crossed lovers.

Train, Cuzco-Puno

I didn't mean to revolve I meant to move.

I didn't know if I was moving myself or letting myself be moved.

I wanted to spread my arms where everything moves through me.

I wanted to expose myself to everything while it exposes itself to me.

I wanted the old incarnation and also the old transcendence.

I wanted all other bodies in mine I wanted all the substance opened I did this

by way of you on a train and while I did I pounded my head

my head my head at yours.

Travel

Something clear, like rain, falling heavily into the black puddle at night.

The slight, frozen surface between us glosses, then our bound one, furious, implicit inside of us.

Train, Cuzco-Puno

Friday the color of gold every beautiful Friday darting, getting out of our way. There is some range of opinion about this Friday—emerging from week's drawer, drawers of these gold mountains. One mountain emerging behind another—small points turned against us. All of our faces lifting and turning through mountains—what we'd give to return—to go back, or to go back in time—the train hits a flock of something. One without a wing, one without a head, feathers everywhere and many birds dying along the tracks as the window passes.

Time travel

When we moved we tried to get at the heavy ghost and to dissolve the heavy ghost and when we did it always looked like one body getting at another body

and they both don't dissolve and the ghost doesn't go anywhere: that is the sound we all make. All getting at one another across the hemispheres

across a history across the body and never actually getting
that is the communal wail.

Would anyone say that: wail, the communal wail of light—turn it down! turn it off!—but then another but then another, another—

The riverboat

Three days down the river almost anything could begin, wanted to begin—

what would a boat have been called on this river before it was called *Oliviera*—

after one sheet of language there is the another sheet upon sheet

which reveals what is behind the faces which reveals what is behind

our face what is behind

fleet upon fleet of boats pulling the rainforest out of itself

then down this river then into the Atlantic—then—does anyone want to say anything

here—

Currency

Here we are in a bus to the port, here we are in a water taxi to another dock upriver, here we are in a van on our way to a tributary river, here we are in his grandmother's tin house waiting for his father to arrive by canoe, here his grandmother has made us sandwiches they are part of the tour package, here we go down to the river behind her house, here is the dock behind her house made out of three planks floating in the water, here is the canoe his father doesn't speak English or Spanish or Portuguese or Quechua but something, here we go from one river to another river to another to another, sometimes the river is more than a mile across, sometimes twenty feet, here we cut through the flooded forest to get to the Orinoco which we can do in this wet season, here the river is so wide in this season that it appears more like a lake, here is the camp and we will stay here for two nights, here his son who drove the van meets us in a motorboat filled with supplies, here is a couple from New Jersey they have been here for two weeks, our package includes a half-day in a canoe in the flooded forest with the father who rows us without speaking through the trees,

here the water so deep in the forest we float halfway up the trunks

here the trees extend so far above our heads that we can barely see the vanishing point

here the reflections of the trees in the water extend so far below us that we can barely see the sky—

here the suspension: the three of us—

here the suspension: that eases the brain that erases the mind when will the light come.

Market

We saw, at our beginning, what is furious

become part of how we would love. Quite a bit of fuss

at this market.

As if we are hemispheres folding onto each other

And where the deepest impressions made. Where

hurt most— you and I are two people who have always wanted to be right. We are two
people who have never wanted to be wrong or to think anything wrong

or to say anything wrong and now all we do is smash continents and bodies together to see
what will remain. Now we try to pull our impression apart from the great impression just to
see if one can

now understand that that great impression is everywhere around us and also inside of us
and we smash smash at each other— like this—to get it out—

Institution

All I can think to do is move and to show myself

hands raised above my head palms open to show—they are empty—to move,

to say I am here, look at my infinity of small,

hidden springs, look at my face—I am susceptible to what you might see,

I am susceptible to what you might say—

Travel

Look: here is the guanabana. Here is the hot milk. Here is a pot of coffee. Here is our fresh bread, look: here is some papaya, here is the granadilla, here is a basket of guava, here is potato soup. Here's another potato, here is a purple potato, here is a blue potato, this black potato looks like Jesus, here is a big cock potato and it likes this pussy potato, finally here is our plantain to go with our favorite throat soup. Here is the cherimoya, here is the jicama and lime, look: let's get some pao de queijo to go with our tiny sweet coffee.

Here is the rice, beans, and manioc, look: our finger bananas, let's get some brigadier after we eat some more throat soup. Here is our roasted cuy, buy some of that lady's empanadas, I'll buy this old guy's fried yucca, look, here is fresh cheese and tamarind jelly, and here's more potato soup. Look: here is my favorite guanabana, you get a bottle of aguardiente, look: Inka Cola, I want much more maracuya, let's get another cheap steak. Here are a dozen tamales, here is our favorite maracuya, here is another hot chocolate, two more bowls of ceviche, look: our favorite guanabana or is that cherimoya, I need that lukewarm beer. Look, here is a tiny cup of coffee, I need another tiny cup of coffee to go with my big shoulder steak.

Travel

I need a cup of coffee why's it so hard to find coffee it's fucking grown here where's the fucking coffee. Are you kidding me Nescafe and white powder?—why don't they drink South American coffee in South America—I'm crying again I have no coffee, twenty hours on a fucking bus and there's no coffee, wait here's a café for tourists they must have some fucking coffee—and you have ordered me three tiny sweet coffees!

Now get me some eggs and bread.

Firmament

On the *Oliviera*, floating slowly down the Amazon, violence attests to what we hold sacred: grunting like sweet baby pigs. The smooth ridges of your gum where the teeth take root. And then the hard pull. Darwin's sea turtles, we know, were stored alive in his pitchblack hull for years—to keep them fresh for the crew while their spices were preserved in oil, as in a baptism fluid—

when we wake, rainbowlight oil in the water spitting out from our engine that is exceeded not even by Noah's.

Market

We bought the most colorful things we could find. Bright red blanket with intricate gold and lime-green stripes. Dark purple sweater. A shawl of black cloth with an orange pattern and a lime-green tablecloth. We covered ourselves with these otherwise we were like nothing. Like organized wind that wanted to keep moving. Moving, like we were so thin with moving. Like it was difficult to locate each other but when we did we asked: are we light—and you—is that light all around you.

Andes

Mostly we moved and moved quietly. And when we were alone with each other.

Outside of the hotel room it was like no one saw us. Inside the room it is winter, a bucket next to the sink for bathing I wash my hair. I dry it with a pillowcase.

We wear all the clothes in our backpacks and get into the bed to get warm.

Like we could never see anyone else like we didn't see each other.

Hypermarket

Irrigation is a magical-thought—under so much water, or so far down. But held—as coca leaves in the hand of a fortune-teller—the spring passed away from us. As pass by us right now the buses, their names painted along their sides. This one, *Angel Mio*. Generation—will it come to mean we tried living alongside one another instead of along the unsplittable cross-grain that a century gives.

Hypermarket

Look: here is the plane from Lima to Bogatá

Here is the plane from Manaus to Salvador de Bahia. Here is the bus to São Paolo. Here is the boat from Leticia to Manaus. Here is the bus from Bogatá to Leticia. Here is the plane from Guayaquil to Lima. The border to Bolivia is closed and here is the train to Juliaca. Here is the bus to Cuzco. Here is the bicycle taxi to the bus station and here is the bus to Quito. Here is the car to the coast of Ecuador. Here is the bus to Cartagena. Here is the van to Tayrona and here is the path we walk for a few miles to the coast. Here is the taxi to the airport. Here the roads in Cartagena are flooding. Here goes our taxi finding alternate routes to the airport and here two homes are floating down the road on our way to the airport. Here the taxi runs some people out of the road and here we have made it to the airport. Here we get on the plane.

Here we go and now we are moving.

Pale

The riverwater smells exactly like Lover. The fog above it floats exactly like we float—we feel very old. We can hardly move ourselves anymore—we feel as old as all the white people taken together. We float. We press in. We moan. We feel very old and we also feel tired.

The ache at the throat. The long press. If I opened it, split it,

would it— does anyone have anything to say—

Covenant

I wear my clothes into the boat's metal shower to wash them with tallow soap. Through the small rectangle hole at eye-level—pampas grass is the beige feathering along the river and beyond it, glowing green fields. Plants truly emit their own light at dusk. At dusk—naked children wash their clothes on the bank. The smell of riverwater is earth rolling over and over.

The water running off me now—is now the river.

On the shore, an Incan stone wall still separates two fields with its pattern of a flower: center stone, five petals. Center stone, petals around.

We are getting tired. Things pass around us or through.

Market

Pushing very hard toward and past each other, pushing their faces forward and the brains behind their faces and their minds inside of those brains and the market hums and the market wails and the market presses and the market is oiled and functioning and the market is brought together with all the animals from all the boats on the river, together with the meat, together with the souvenirs and all the women who sell us things while holding their children, and all together and the market gave us food. The market gave us luggage. The market gave us the blankets within which we touch each other.

Sphinx

You, woman selling cloth at the market—I like to think of you as someone I can buy
something from. And your little girl asleep beside you—I like to think of her as my—
with what material do I attach myself to you—with ghosts thickened up into money,
money thickened up into bodies thickened up into information and information
thickened to—hold my attention—hold my attention—

you won't be able to love it—

do you want to say something here.

Learning history

First the mountain, then the word, then the market, then the Indian. First the boat then the river then the floor of the river there the fossil. There the fossil there the oil, there the oil there the ghost. There the ghost there the bishop fucking the archbishop fucking the senator. There the senator there the blanket there the bank there the school. There the school there the cathedral there the cathedral here the bones. There the bones there the CEO there the CEO there free trade zone there the free trade zone here the ghost. There the ghost there the light. There the light there the bank account routing number. There the bank account routing number there the ATM there the tourist there the bus. There the tourist there the market there the market there the Indian with his potatoes with his blankets with his children down from the mountain.

Meridian

There: exactly there. The little panels, the curtains—the machines—there we are.

Excelling violet

Unlocked at the plastic—the legs, folded against the mirror

and the mirror glued to the inside of the lid and on the top of the lid is a picture of the gold path

and the lid open or shut will determine whether the song—the crank—

the spring deep at her

and also the jinx

and also the solution and also the snare—.

Excelling violet

If color is waves across space and time and if waves have no mass.

If waves have no mass then they have no weight then color is doing not being—

But if waves cannot unfold all their folds at once—

but if folds are atoms and atoms are crypts and upon the crypts are written—.

But if—as they approach each other—the writing in the crypt does change—

if—as we approach each other—gravity does bend

the light.

Firmament

We were touching each other, of course.

What we didn't know then was the rushing quiet of lakes below ice—who knows about that?

I believed, also, in other actions—sockets of ice and long plateaus of ice with their desperations—and we thought, what's done is still doing. No matter what you will give to be sure of being loved by this whole world—they'll take some and slide back through the glacial bars, into that formal black lake. Please, keep finding me. I have found you, fallen a long way. Falling against your own mother. And afterward, you are small.

Spring—

Sometimes we hate what we do altogether so then we try to become transparent. Then we try to become opaque. Then we try to be quiet and to fold or to spread or to spill ourselves out but there's nowhere—

everywhere we go, we exist and existed before. Covenant, promise, treaty, pact: the words diminish the words extend too far so why would I promise you anything—oath, vow, contract, trade route, landing strip, shipping lane—

trajectory—could we have traveled and in doing so, hurt nothing.

Could we have remained very still—so still like the meditators say and the trajectory becomes a single point or something else—and in doing so—hurt nothing.

Move so far or remain so still and the blanket of language lifts and a single word that means anything like *believe me* emerges that we could say it—language, between us

exposed before opening.

Iris

Trying to reach toward something lifting and lowering us across the world and asking are the eyes stuck in the body. Is the institution stuck in the body. Is the language stuck in the mind and then the mind stuck in the brain.

Maybe as easy as something I could remove of my body. An organ removed. A ghost exorcised or something hard, something—a medallion somewhere probably inside me encrusted—pried off.

And when it is—.

Rustling, so beautifully?   Galactic roses.

It's months now and no one has touched either of us except each other. The more we are traveling white lovers the less we can touch anyone else. I want touching others and say to them touch me. Take my money and touch me. When I hand this to you touch my finger, touch even my wrist and at the market touch me in the crowd, rub some part of this money. You're pissed at my doubt in the garden where greener *I-don't-know* roses take care of people, with no debt of caring. The roses, nevertheless—(I will take care of you/ you will take care of me —).

Hammer buried in white mud, bank of the Orinoco

We move slowly across the continent, up and down,

across and diagonally, in boats and in airplanes,

in trains, in cars, in bicycle taxis, in buses.

We are feeling good. We aren't hurting anyone.

We are feeling good. We aren't hurting anyone.

Everywhere we go, our minds think, we aren't hurting anyone.

Economy

I have an idea and I come here and it is confirmed. I have many sets of ideas and I come here and they shuffle slightly. I have no ideas and I have unstable ideas and I have ideas that repulse me and so I come here and I forget them and we float down the river.

We try not to be reminders for each other of those bad ideas. We try to expose ourselves to fresh ideas

and the ideas below that and ideas below that—someone was here before us—

am I talking to you—are we talking to each other—am I relating ideas.

The coca leaf fortune-teller

A half-dome of fallen wheat against our diminishing belief in any kind of marriage.

The coca leaf fortune-teller

Your spine stretched along the roof of a boat. This boat of Santa's black paint, Darwin's drop, Noah's imbecile raven, and Basho's fleeting lope—but I wished from the river a more labyrinthine curvature—wished any solid, fetal curl nestled to a hinging frame, wished for the hinge and for the pivot between—

wished *curl* and wished *bend* and wished *arc*—which way.

Which way next.

Do you want to say anything here.

Would you say Manaus lies at the confluence of the Rio Negro and the Rio Solimões—

where the black and white rivers meet. Would you say history of Manaus.

Would you say years that hunch themselves between—

would you call this remembering.

Would you ask: did the garden become a market. And did the mountain

become a station. Did the route become the thread

you say in this twenty-thousand pesos bill—here you show me

there are snowflakes. Here you show me is the violet labyrinth.

Here on the other side of this money you say is earth stamped with a thumbprint pattern.

Oliviera

This morning, rainbowlight-cerebellums in the arc of water that is spitting

out from the engine.

Floating turd next to the dead floating snake

Near Manaus the black and white rivers meet, run separately in two colors, then blend toward the sea. Your nightmare at The Hotel Continental—below a chandelier at the confluence of massacre. Our window overlooks the plumbing for the hotel's latrines—a creaturely plastic piping straight into the river. My dream, in Manaus, of a hatchet to my skull—its tip, wedging gently open, and that relief.

Ghost

When ghosts love each other it becomes difficult to tell them apart

and that's what we wanted. We wanted, like the clouds, to be general. We wanted to be light lost within all the light. We wanted, like stars, to be held in the general dark. I wanted, I said, not to bear

this single ghost everywhere I went. I was sorry, everywhere, to lay this ghost bare—

Thread

We float through this canyon of melted rock where earth unfurls to its reddest scale. Mantle, opened then spread for the line of gigantic reflective white jesuses marking cliff to peak to valley to city—cement christs breaking the line of the more ancient Incan map—

breaking the veil of ravens darkening the sunset, darkening the route. Listen: the grandmother told us *Be careful what you think when you travel this river—your thoughts like the current will become the path.*

What we think when we travel this river

Hundreds of hammocks are hung so close that the wake of other boats taps us into one another. Into the old lovers hanging just inches above, into the very young family right beside, into the soon-to-be lovers just below. The boat rocks gently and all the hammocks sway all day, all night. The television is still full-volume and motorcycles and gunshots at Lover's head—the boat rocks—all the hammocks sway, touch, part—sway, touch, part. We touch other people all day, all night and no one is hurt. We are touched by other people all day, all night, and we are not hurt.

Firmament

Inside of myself, I told him, there is no light at all. Light penetrates

nowhere in there. Here, the unborn child

is referred to as light. They ask us—but don't touch us—wherever we go

When will the light come? The baby next to us suckles and punches—

he has the perfect baby-life. A vermillion poncho

and in the morning his whole family shares from one large bowl.

What we think when we travel this river

We think when will the light come. We think

how turn off the light.

We fuck and contemplate down the river—

the river profound the river echoing with television.

Our fucking in the hammock hidden by our blanket just like everyone else's fucking just inches

from ours is hidden by their blankets and we think

there is something inside of us.

We are slamming are digging at something

that is inside of everyone that wants to hide from a screaming light.

Sunset, Tayrona

Smelling you, especially at evening: gradations of sex and of sheltering across the mica beach where we will sleep. The moon is a root of fire. A very little light in the sky—dark blue, as the metal ripening silently to gold in some deep mine.

The seven directions

Lover holds my head, a finger in my ear—(a shred, hyacinth-white, a cloth)—those resolving images seal the angel-shaped bloodstain, size of a butterfly, when I stand. There is color fallen, after all, from inside me. My recollection of his arms, brilliantly, the moon's lintel.

Night, Tayrona

The sky is black air with stars all across it.

The beach is black sand with flecks of mica mixed through it.

The beach and the sky are identical and full of light.

Lying there—the sound of the tide

galactic—

suspended in outer space—whitish stains on the black, but the minds and the bodies have gone.

The coca leaf fortune-teller

The old woman threw a chicken bone from her soup our way. Her blanket spread out on the train-rail, used-electronics for sale. The muddy ice… steam rises from her soup with the habañero in the pot for warmth. Her little granddaughter shits in a red plastic bucket behind her.

Star-shaped hubcaps across Medellín

The iris, starless at its heart—grows in the medicine wheel of demolished black birds that dropped around us— you see, what we create might not save us. This turned-hard year— hanging banana tree flower, its sexual lobe is a cultigen that couldn't run wild. We move, we are quiet, we lay ourselves together on everything.

Iris, starless

Yet if my ghost.

Yet if my money. Yet if the proscenium arch—or

if the firmament—yet if gel paper yet if on the ark—yet

if my mind— like the peepholes in the eyelet curtains

hung in this bus named *Jesucristo*—

yet if tracing each other. Yet if situated yet if infinite.

Yet acoustic yet if pyrotechnic.

If infinite pyrotechnics.

Or to say—

The olive branch. The seven directions—children, selling us something everywhere we go. Speckled fish in the hand of a little proprietor, her pink plastic flip-flops. Fireflies over our hammock. Mica from the beach in her braid, she has woken us to sell us the birdbaths she's made from shell. To sell us the fish and the water.

To sell us the thatch-roof, the retaining wall, the load-bearing wall.

Iris

When the *Oliviera* moved us down the river, above the river, every morning, the fog. In the fog, periodically, a misshapen rainbow blown alongside us for a while, keeping apace the boat.

Or, if the light hits it just so, misshapen rainbow in the oil floating alongside the boat. Oil from her engine that moved us.

Ghost

Oil that moves *Angel Mio*. Oil that moves *Salve Regina*. Oil that moves *Espíritu Santo*. The oil that moves *Arco Iris* across the continent as does the

oil that moves this plane again, and we, also enraged or throbbing fly over this continent still in the blanket also smashing, frothing across the continent—

Ruins

A burro is asleep on the porch beside the war-painted tricycle. The ancient Incan agricultural test-fields are still terraced down the mountain behind us, their spring at the peak translates as *No Origin*. This one is a slow, mint-green river. Alongside it, wheat fields. Piles of that wheat are spread across the valley's road for the cars and buses to thresh—.

You say, Did you say a warping tricycle? You say, Where are we now. You say, What do you think about that?

Suspension

After swimming in the water that lit us like flame and then hid us—

after our canoe through the flooded forest and the sky so far above us and the sky so far below us and the trees extending to a vanishing point in every direction—

after the mica beach in outer space—after blue light—chambers—after all that fucking after all that moving were there moments we faced—

or is it this: were there moments we were faced

or is it this: were there moments our bodies or minds stood in for

or is it this: were there moments actual light

or is it this: were there moments facing each other

or is it this: faceless—

Ghost

What I remember of that dancer is this: she revolved and bent over and eventually she stopped twirling but she never moved out of the box. And the gold key—I almost immediately lost it. It is a stupid memory, it was a stupid song.

It is the worst-possible thing to have loved.

The coca leaf fortune-teller

Is there anything you want to say here—.

That we are all eating this blue animal together. That we're all clutching this blue animal together

Does anyone have anything to say—that after all this, light is still just light.

That every single bit of it comes from exactly the same old fireball.

That darkness on the other hand seems to come from almost everywhere that darkness

holds us that darkness is what is inside of us where—did anyone touch anyone else—

what do you think about that.

What are we supposed to think about that.

Other Saturnalia books:

Nowhere Fast by William Kulik

The Girls of Peculiar by Catherine Pierce

Xing by Debora Kuan

Other Romes by Derek Mong

Faulkner's Rosary by Sarah Vap

Gurlesque: the new grrly, grotesque, burlesque poetics
edited by Lara Glenum and Arielle Greenberg

Tsim Tsum by Sabrina Orah Mark

Hush Sessions by Kristi Maxwell

Days of Unwilling by Cal Bedient

Letters to Poets: Conversations about Poetics, Politics, and Community
edited by Jennifer Firestone and Dana Teen Lomax

Artist/Poet Collaboration Series:
Velleity's Shade by Star Black / Artwork by Bill Knott
Polytheogamy by Timothy Liu / Artwork by Greg Drasler
Midnights by Jane Miller / Artwork by Beverly Pepper
Stigmata Errata Etcetera by Bill Knott / Artwork by Star Black
Ing Grish by John Yau / Artwork by Thomas Nozkowski
Blackboards by Tomaz Salamun / Artwork by Metka Krasovec

Winners of the Saturnalia Books Poetry Prize:
My Scarlet Ways by Tanya Larkin
The Little Office of the Immaculate Conception by Martha Silano
Personification by Margaret Ronda
To the Bone by Sebastian Agudelo
Famous Last Words by Catherine Pierce
Dummy Fire by Sarah Vap
Correspondence by Kathleen Graber
The Babies by Sabrina Orah Mark

Arco Iris I was printed using the fonts Lucida Sans and AGaramond.

www.saturnaliabooks.org